ENVIRONMENTAL ISSUES

AGRICULTURE AND LAND USE

By Emilie Dufresne

KidHaven PUBLISHING

Published in 2020 by
KidHaven Publishing, an Imprint of Greenhaven Publishing, LLC
353 3rd Avenue
Suite 255
New York, NY 10010

© 2020 Booklife Publishing

This edition is published by arrangement with Booklife Publishing

Edited by: Holly Duhig
Designed by: Amy Li

Cataloging-in-Publication Data

Names: Dufresne, Emilie.
Title: Agriculture and land use / Emilie Dufresne.
Description: New York : KidHaven Publishing, 2020. | Series: Environmental issues | Includes glossary and index.
Identifiers: ISBN 9781534530713 (pbk.) | ISBN 9781534530324 (library bound) | ISBN 9781534531642 (6 pack) | ISBN 9781534530591 (ebook)
Subjects: LCSH: Agriculture--Juvenile literature. | Land use--Juvenile literature.
Classification: LCC S493.D847 2020 | DDC 630--dc23

Printed in the United States of America

CPSIA compliance information: Batch #BS19KL: For further information contact Greenhaven Publishing LLC, New York, New York at 1-844-317-7404.

Please visit our website, www.greenhavenpublishing.com. For a free color catalog of all our high-quality books, call toll free 1-844-317-7404 or fax 1-844-317-7405.

Words that look like **this** can be found in the glossary on page 24.

Photo credits – Images are courtesy of Shutterstock.com. With thanks to Getty Images, Thinkstock Photo and iStockphoto. Cover – DK Arts, 1 – Sergey Logrus , 2 – LALS STOCK, 3 – Ortodox, 4 – Fotokostic, 5 – Ewa Studio, 6 – YuRi Photolife, 7 – asharkyu, 8 – alexmisu, 9 – Leah-Anne Thompson, 10 – Ten03, 11 – CHURN, 12 – Jinning Li, 13 – Nikolay Gyngazov, 14 – FUN FUN PHOTO, 15 – Vlad Teodor, 16 – kropic1, 17 – Orientaly, 18 – Kokliang, 19 – Marten, 20 – smereka, 21 – Rich Carey, 22 – Pikul Noorod, 23 – MarjanCermelj, M-SUR.

CONTENTS

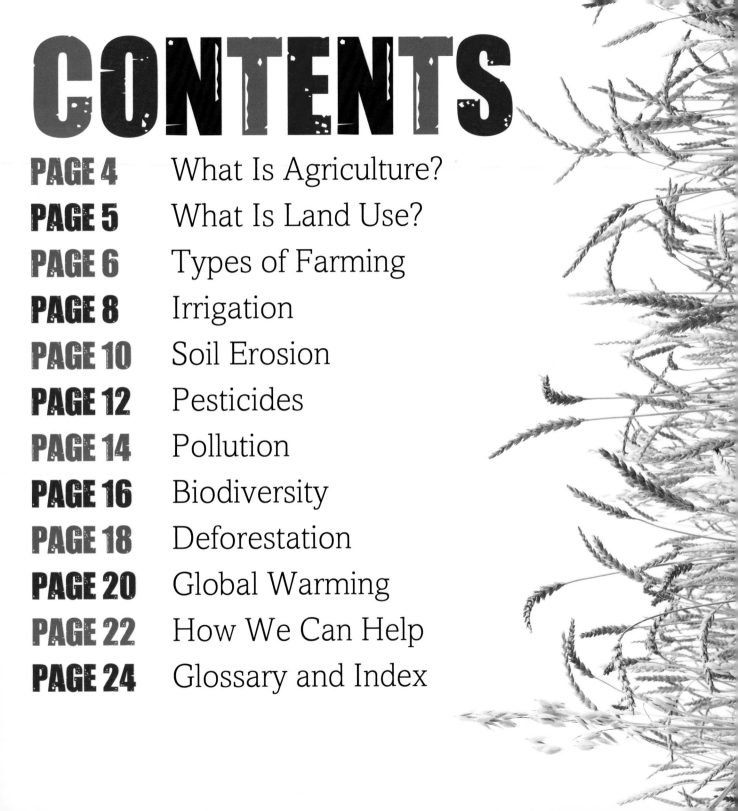

WHAT IS AGRICULTURE?

Agriculture is the way we use the land to grow food and **rear** animals. It is also known as farming. It refers to everything we do to create food. For plants, this means preparing the soil, planting the seeds, and harvesting the **crops**.

WHAT IS LAND USE?

Land use is the way we use and change different types of land so farming can take place. For example, a forest might be cut down to create a farm to rear animals or a field to grow crops.

TYPES OF FARMING

There are lots of different ways that we can farm plants. Lots of plants are grown outside in fields. Some plants are grown indoors or in greenhouses. Greenhouses let us grow crops that usually wouldn't grow in cold weather.

LETTUCE GROWING HYDROPONICALLY

Another way we can farm plants is hydroponically. This type of farming doesn't use soil. Instead, plants are grown in water. This means the plants are less likely to get sick or die, because they are in a **controlled environment**.

IRRIGATION

Agriculture can cause a lot of environmental issues. Some of these issues are caused by irrigation. Irrigated areas have pipes that help to water the field.

THIS MEANS FARMERS DON'T HAVE TO WORRY ABOUT THEIR CROPS GETTING TOO LITTLE WATER.

IRRIGATION MAY BE GOOD FOR FARMERS AND THEIR CROPS, BUT IS BAD FOR THE ENVIRONMENT.

Over time, irrigation can take water away from areas that need it, such as rivers and lakes. This means that lots of animal **habitats** are lost. Irrigation can also cause **waterlogging**.

SOIL EROSION

Farmers **plow** their fields to make planting easier. This leaves a layer of loose soil on the ground called topsoil, which is sometimes taken away by wind or rain. This is called soil erosion.

TOPSOIL BEING ERODED BY THE WIND

When topsoil is eroded, the land that is left has fewer **nutrients** in it. Soil erosion also stops the ground from storing water. This makes it harder for crops to grow in the soil.

PESTICIDES

Pesticides are **chemicals** that are sprayed on crops to protect them from bugs and diseases. This can be a good thing, because it helps farmers produce more food for us to eat.

Pesticides may help farmers, but they aren't good for the environment. When pesticides are sprayed, lots of the chemicals are released into the air. The pesticides are spread by the wind and can harm other plants, rivers, and animals.

THESE CHEMICALS ARE DANGEROUS TO WILDLIFE AND ANIMALS.

POLLUTION

Agriculture and land use create a lot of different types of pollution. The farm machinery can be very loud and create noise pollution. The factories that process the food create a lot of light pollution.

SCIENTISTS TESTING POLLUTED SOIL

If the chemicals in pesticides are not looked after properly, they can build up in the soil and cause soil pollution. When soil becomes polluted, it can cause water and air pollution as well.

BIODIVERSITY

FORESTS LIKE THIS ONE HAVE LOTS OF BIODIVERSITY.

If a place has a lot of biodiversity, it means that it has many different animals and plants living there. Having lots of biodiversity is important to keep the environment healthy.

Forests are often cut down to make more space to grow crops and rear animals. This is called deforestation. This can lead to less biodiversity because there is less space for different animals and plants to live.

MANY FARMS ONLY GROW ONE TYPE OF CROP IN EACH FIELD.

DEFORESTATION

Forests are a very important part of the environment because the trees provide the planet with the **oxygen** that humans and animals need to live. Forests are also home to many animals and plants.

RAIN FORESTS ONLY COVER AROUND 2 PERCENT OF THE WORLD'S SURFACE, BUT ARE HOME TO 50 PERCENT OF THE WORLD'S PLANT AND ANIMAL SPECIES.

DEFORESTATION CONTRIBUTES TO CLIMATE CHANGE.

Forests are cut down to make space for crops to be grown.
This means that lots of animal and plant homes are destroyed.
It also means that there aren't as many plants to create
the oxygen that animals need to breathe.

GLOBAL WARMING

The earth is getting warmer and warmer – this is called global warming. It is partly caused by **greenhouse gases** being released into the air. Farming releases a lot of greenhouse gases, such as **methane**.

ONE COW CAN MAKE BETWEEN 155 POUNDS (70 KG) AND 265 POUNDS (120 KG) OF METHANE EACH YEAR!

Plants and trees absorb greenhouse gases and release oxygen. This means that when trees are cut down to make space for farming, lots of greenhouse gases are released into the air.

HOW WE CAN HELP

ORGANIC FOOD

Organic crops are food products that are grown without using synthetic, or nonnatural, pesticides. This means fewer chemicals are released into the environment.

GROW YOUR OWN

You can try growing your own fruit and vegetables, such as tomatoes, carrots, and strawberries. That way, you get to eat tasty food and know that it hasn't harmed the environment.

CHECK THE LABEL

Deforestation occurs to make room to grow products like palm oil. When you go shopping with your parents, check the label. Try to get food without palm oil.

BUILDING BIODIVERSITY

Build a bug hotel or plant flowers to increase biodiversity. You can use toilet paper tubes, flowerpots, and sticks to make bug hotels.

GLOSSARY

chemicals	substances that are usually made by scientists
controlled environment	a man-made environment that is looked after
crops	plants that are grown on a large scale to be eaten or used
greenhouse gases	gases in the atmosphere that trap the sun's heat
habitats	the natural environments in which animals or plants live
hydroponically	growing plants in liquid, sand, or gravel that contains all the things they need to grow
methane	a gas with no color or smell
nutrients	natural substances that plants and animals need to grow and stay healthy
oxygen	a natural gas that all animals need in order to survive
plow	to turn over the soil, leaving it ready for planting seeds
rear	to breed and raise an animal for a particular use or purpose
waterlogging	when the soil is so full of water that extra water sits on top of the ground

INDEX